SCHIRMER'S LIBRARY
OF MUSICAL CLASSICS

CARL CZERNY

Selected Studies

For the Piano

AN ANTHOLOGY

Selected and Edited by
LOUIS OESTERLE

IN FOUR BOOKS

→ Book I — Vol. 994   Book III — Vol. 996

Book II — Vol. 995   Book IV — Vol. 997

G. SCHIRMER, *Inc.*

DISTRIBUTED BY

HAL•LEONARD®
CORPORATION

7777 W. BLUEMOUND RD. P.O. BOX 13819 MILWAUKEE, WI 53213

CONTENTS

→ VOLUME I

Selected Studies

For the Piano

AN ANTHOLOGY

Anthology of Czerny Piano-Studies
Part I
One Hundred Short Studies
selected from
Op. 66, 139, 261, 300, 453, 501, 599, 792, 820, 821 and 848

19246

Printed in the U.S.A.

4

4. Allegro

5. Allegro

6. Allegro moderato

7. Allegro

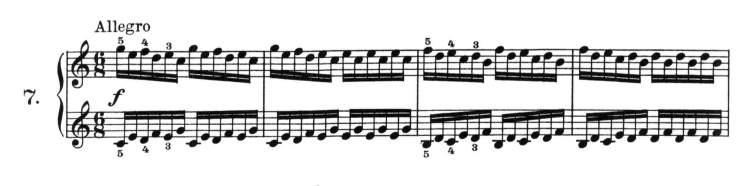

Allegro

8.

Allegretto

9.

Allegretto

10.

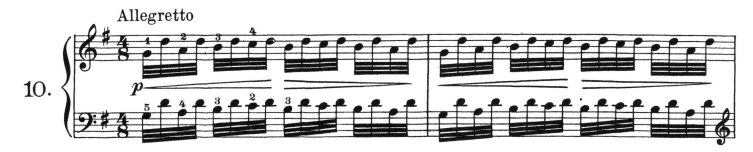

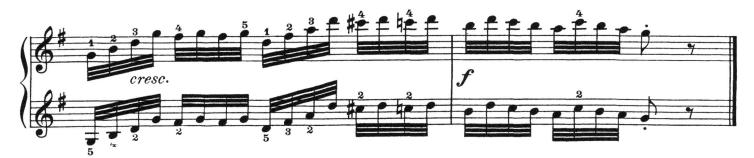

11.

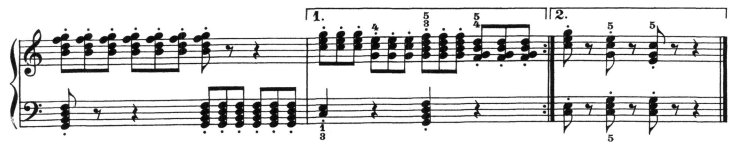

12.

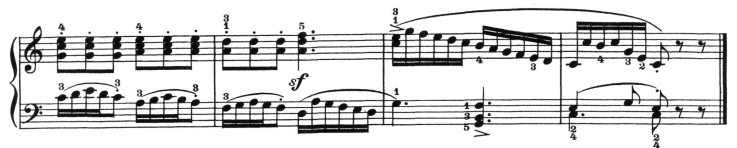

13.

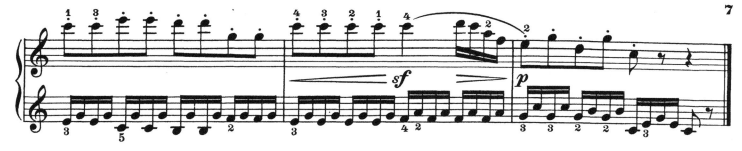

Allegro

14.

Allegretto

15.

19.

Allegro

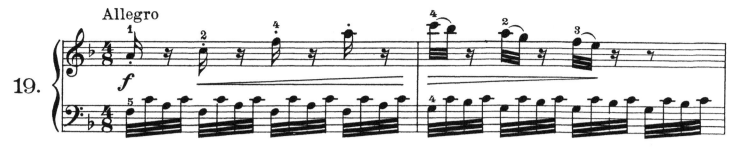

20.

Allegro vivace

Allegro

23.

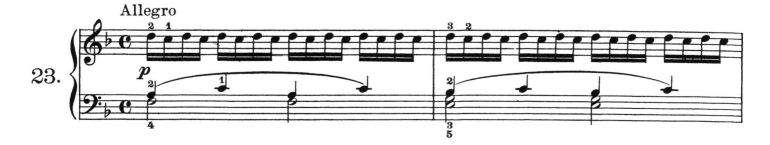

Allegro

24.

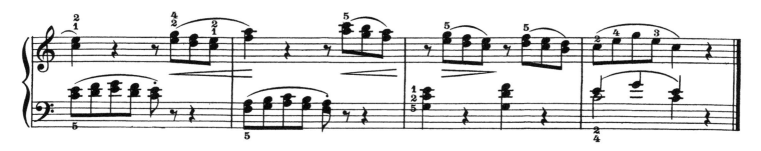

Allegretto animato

25.

Allegretto

26.

Allegro

27.

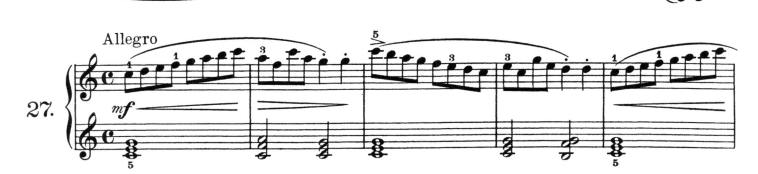

28.

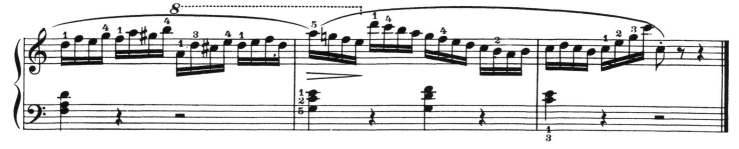

29.

Allegro

30.

Allegro moderato

31.

Scale of C Major

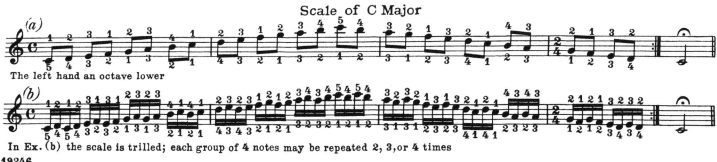

The left hand an octave lower

In Ex. (b) the scale is trilled; each group of 4 notes may be repeated 2, 3, or 4 times

19246

Allegro vivace

32.

Allegro veloce

33.

19246

Veloce

34.

Allegretto vivace

35.

Allegretto

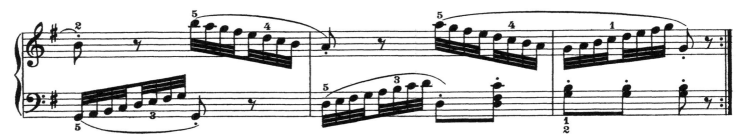

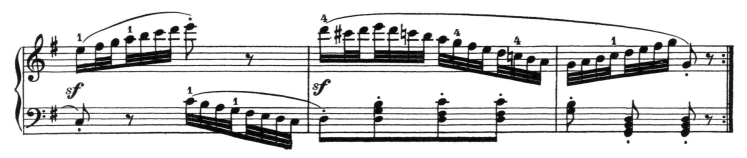

★ The original is in C major.

Molto allegro

37.

Allegretto

38.

19246

Presto

39.

Common Chords Founded on the C major Scale

C major   D minor   E minor   F major   G major   A minor   B diminished

The left hand plays two octaves lower.
Arpeggiate all these chords as shown on the next page.
Practise also with omission of the highest note of each chord.

Allegretto

40.

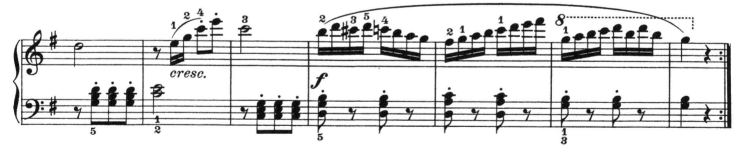

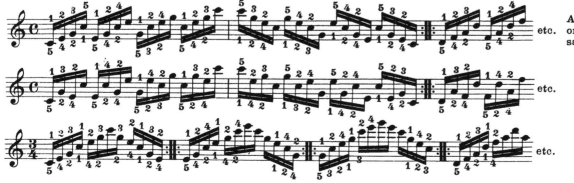

Arpeggiate the other chords on preceding page in the same manner.

41.

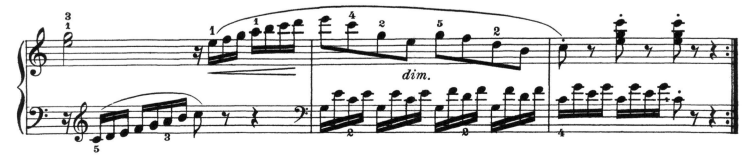

Allegro molto

42.

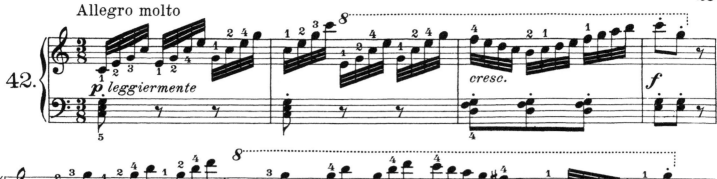

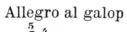

Allegro al galop

43.

Molto allegro
(*Prelude*)

44.

Allegro

45.

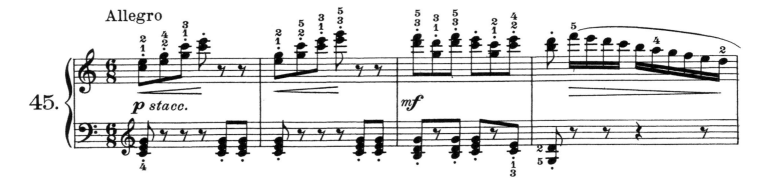

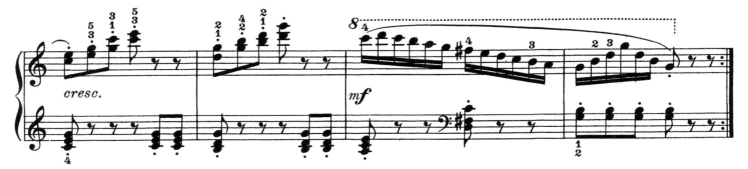

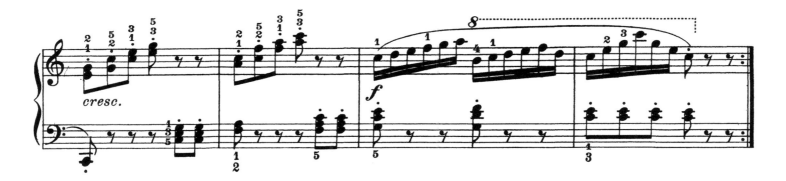

Allegro vivo e scherzando

46.

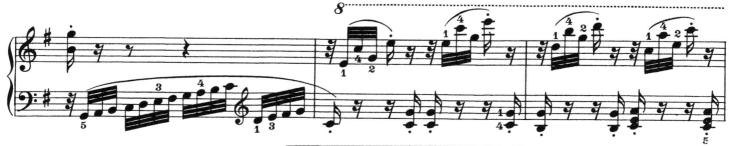

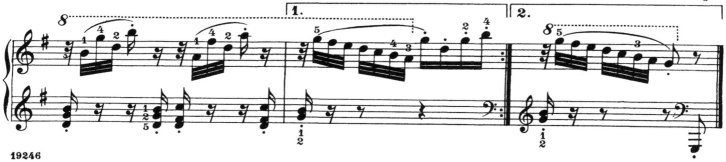

28

Allegro

47.*

* The original is in C major.
19246

Allegro vivace

48.

* The original is in C minor.

Lento

49.

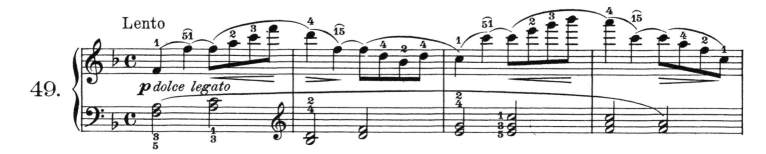

Allegretto all'Ungherese

50.

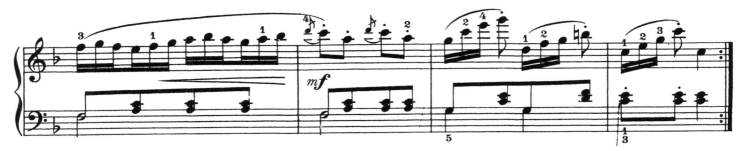

Allegro vivace
(Prelude)

51.

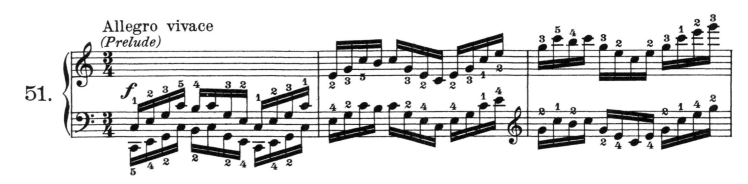

Molto allegro
(Prelude)

52.

Allegro

53.

Allegro

54.

Allegro

55.

Moderato

56.

Allegro moderato

57.

Allegro vivo

60.

Allegro

61.

62.

Allegro vivace

63.

Allegro

64.

Allegro comodo

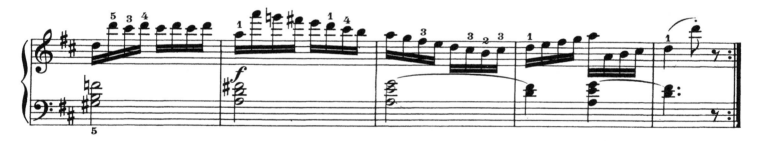

Allegro

65.

Allegretto

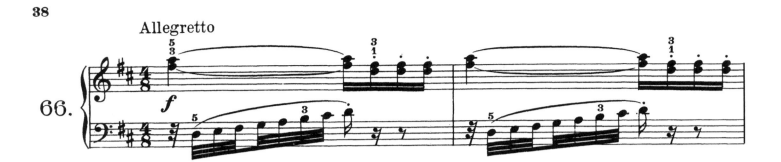

66.

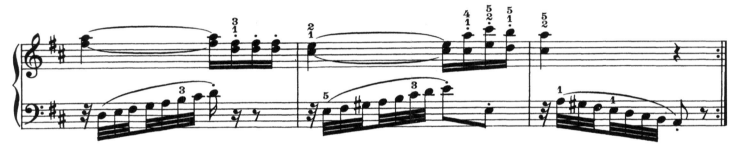

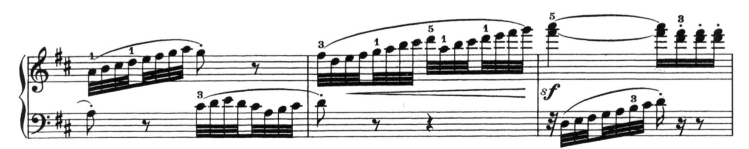

Allegro veloce

67.

Variant 1

69a

Variant 2

69b

Allegro

70.

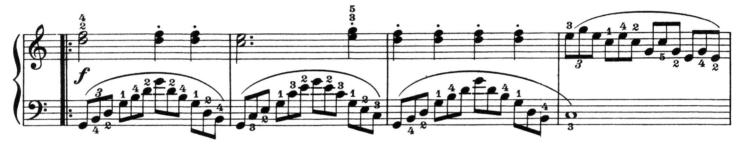

* Also transpose a semitone higher and lower.

Allegro

71.

19246

Allegro vivo energico

72.

Allegro

73.

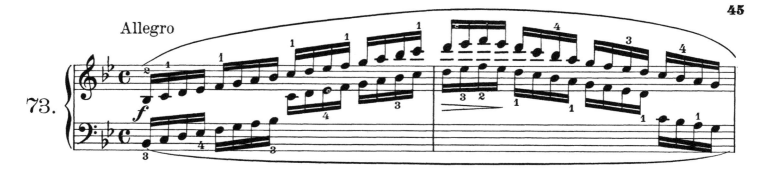

Allegro moderato

74.

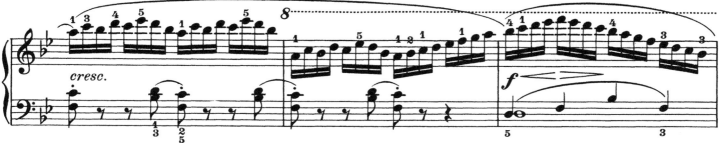

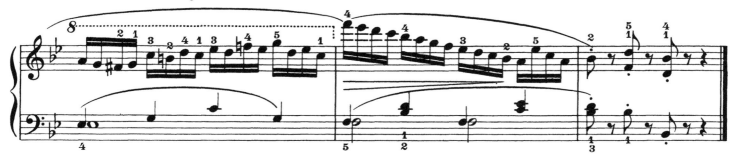

Allegro

75.

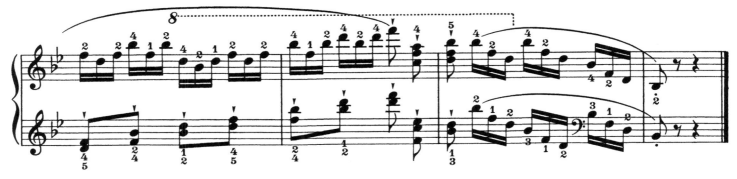

Allegretto

76.

Allegro moderato

77.

Allegro vivace

78.

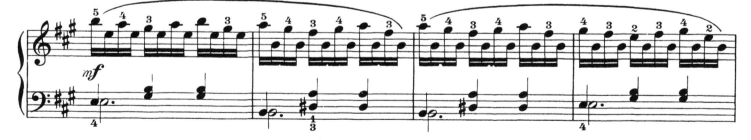

D. C. al Fine

Allegro vivo

79.

Dominant Seventh-chord in C Major

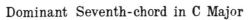

Left hand an octave lower

Allegretto

Diminished Seventh-chords

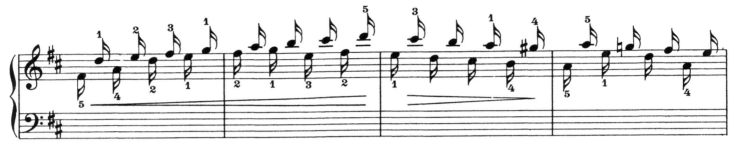

Exercises

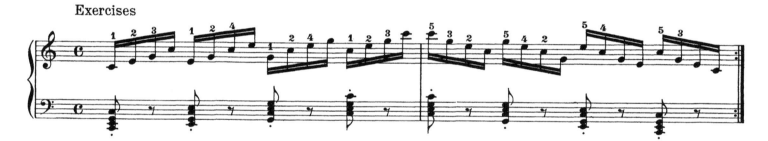

Allegro

82.

Allegro moderato

83.

Allegro moderato

84.

Allegro vivace

85.

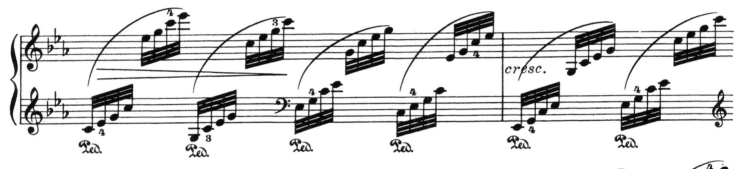

*Variant for Chord-practice

l.h. r.h. l.h. r.h.

etc.

This Study may also be changed
into C major by playing only on
white keys

87.

88.

Allegretto animato

dolce scherzoso

Allegro

Chromatic Scale

(l.h. an octave lower)

Allegro

89.

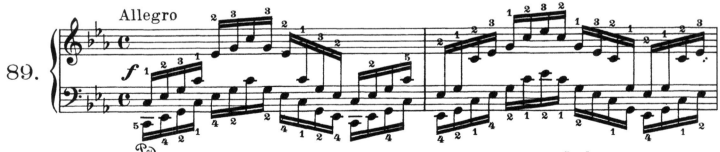

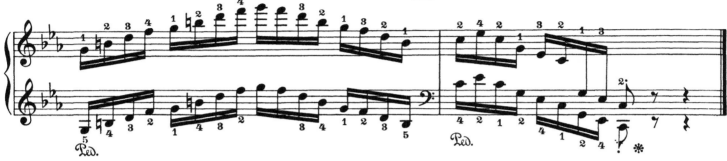

Allegro

90.

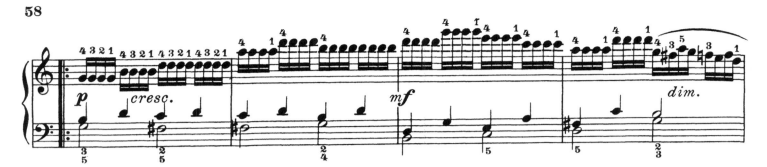

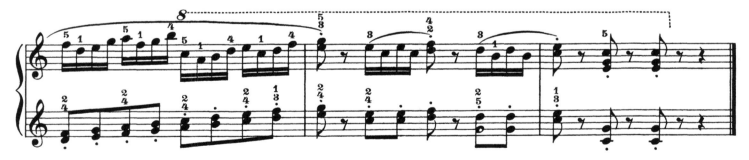

Andante grazioso

92.

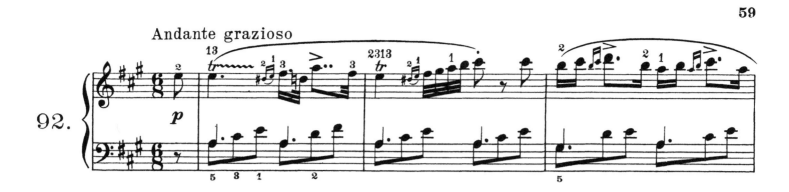

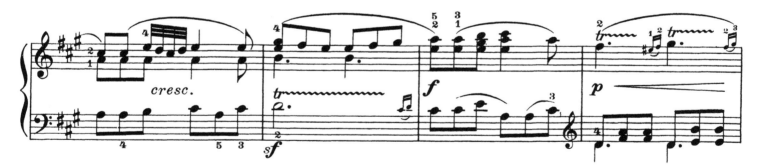

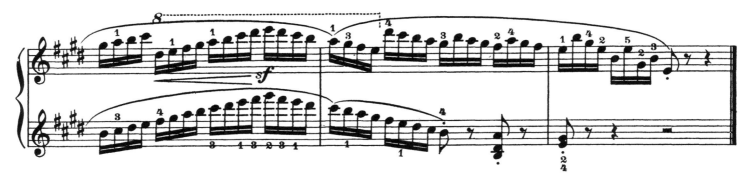

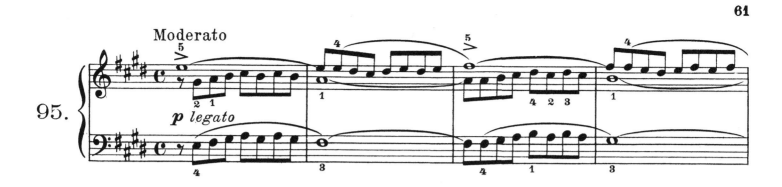

95.

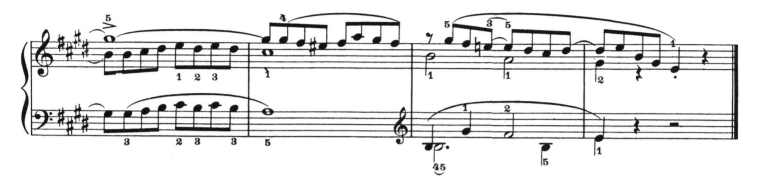

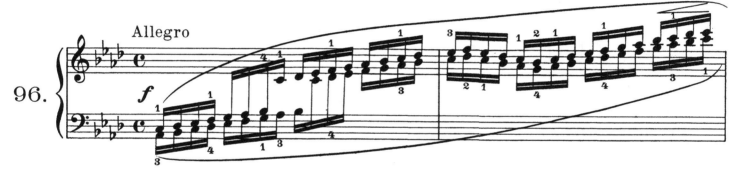

96.

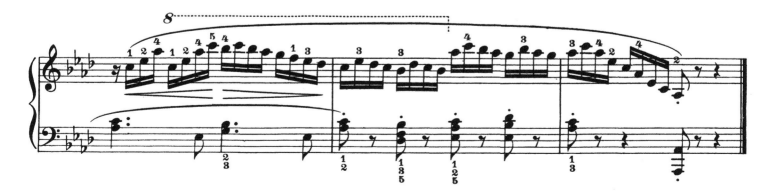

Allegro vivace

97.

legato sempre

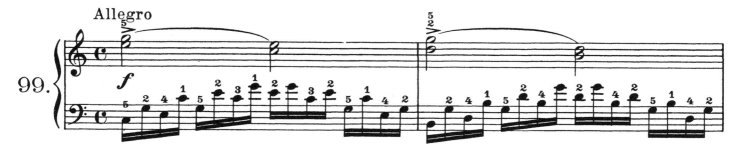

Allegretto vivace

100.

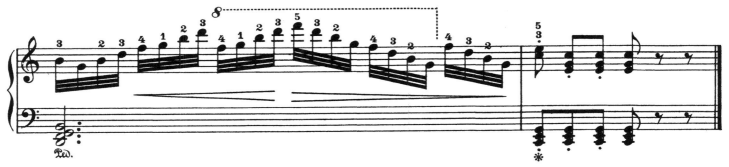

Exercises

Anthology of Czerny Piano-Studies

Part II

Seventy Studies

selected from

Op. 261, 335, 453, 636, 748, 749, 807, 818, 821, 829, 848 and 849

*) The left hand may practise the right-hand part two octaves lower, either alone or with the right hand. Ed.

19246

Preparatory Pedal-Exercises

At (a) the common, simple, and most advantageous manner of adding pedal-signs to a composition, directly under a note or chord, is indicated. It simply shows that the note or chord under which the sign stands should be sustained by the pedal. When the pedalling is indicated thus, it is assumed that the player knows how to use the pedal, that is, in a syncopated manner, as shown at (b), the foot pressing the pedal down on the dotted eighth-notes, and releasing it on the sixteenth-rests. (Compare Study No. 35.) Ed.

Molto allegro (♩ = 100)

3.

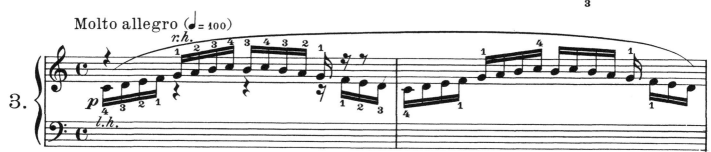

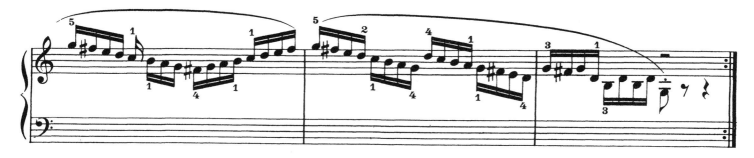

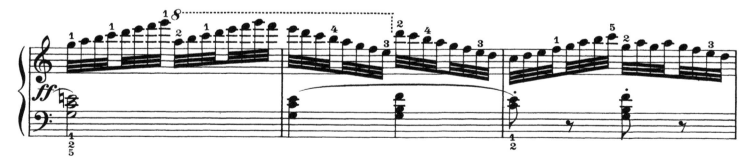

19246

Allegro non troppo

5.

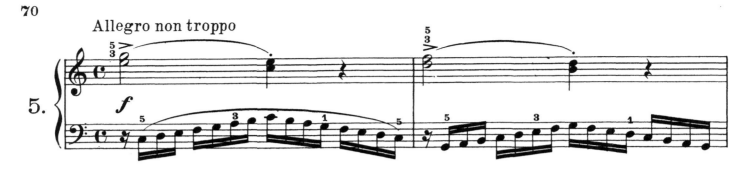

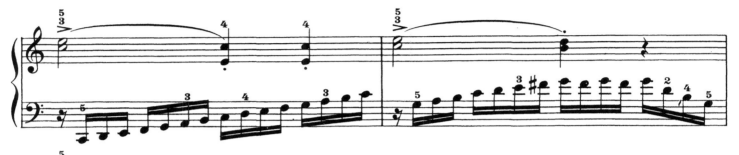

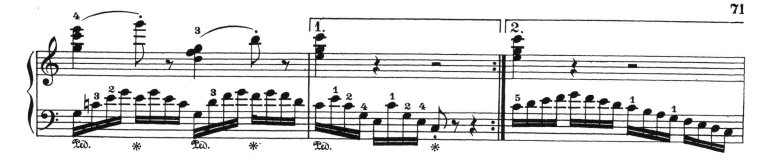

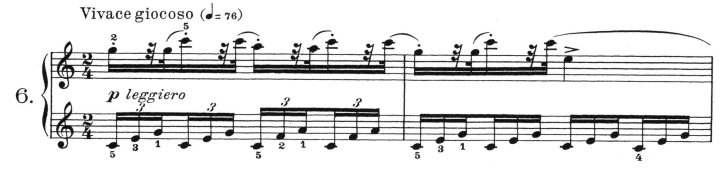

Vivace giocoso (♩ = 76)

6.

Allegro non troppo (♩ = 72)
sempre legato sino alla fine

7.

Allegro ($\quad = 144$)

legato

8.

Allegro non troppo

9.

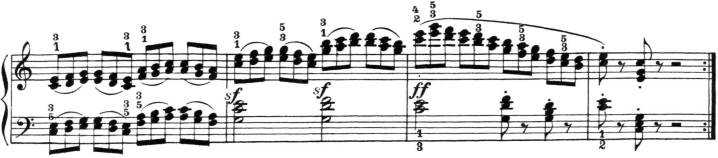

Allegro

12:

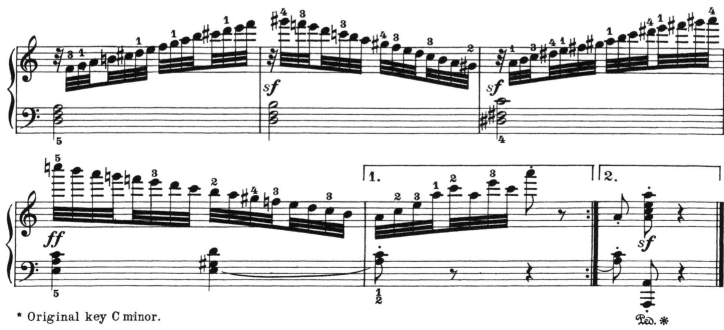

* Original key C minor.

19246

Molto vivace (♩=80)

13.

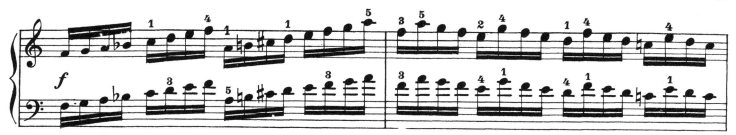

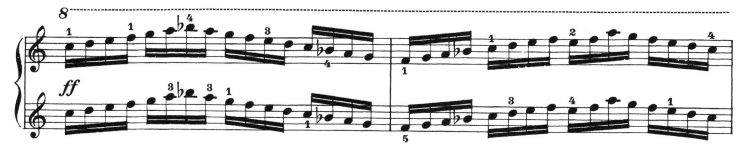

Allegro vivace ($\bullet$.=88)

14.

19246

Molto vivace (♩. = 60)

15.

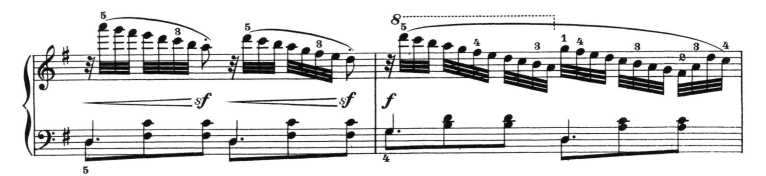

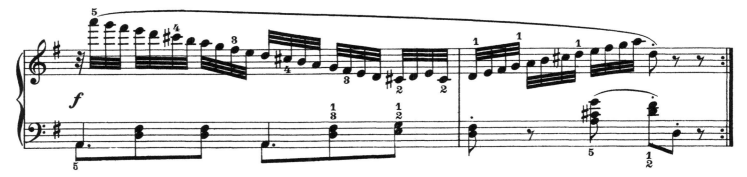

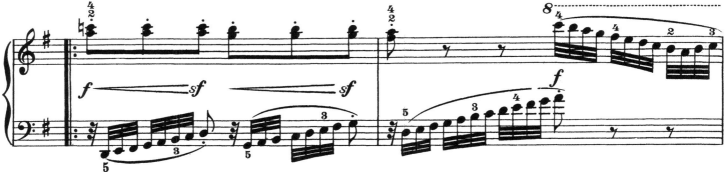

16.

Allegretto vivace (♩= 80)

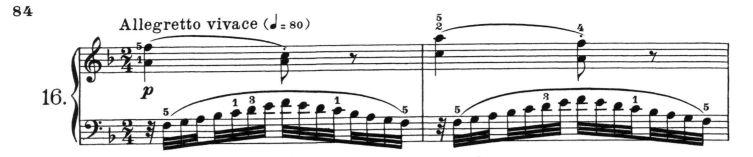

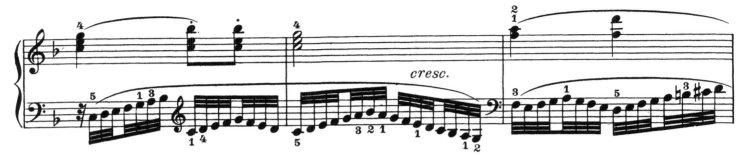

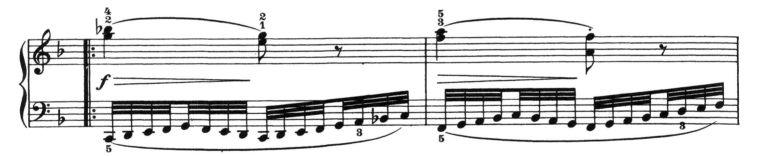

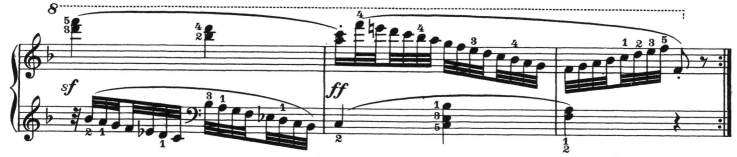

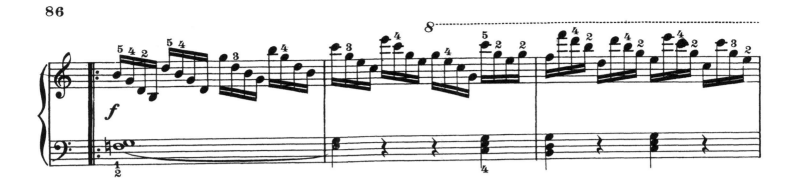

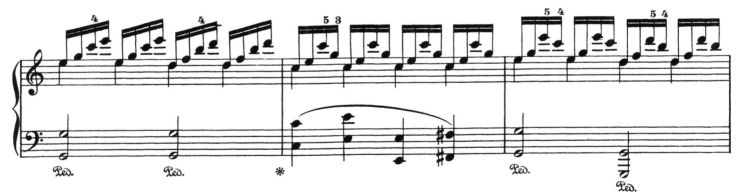

18.

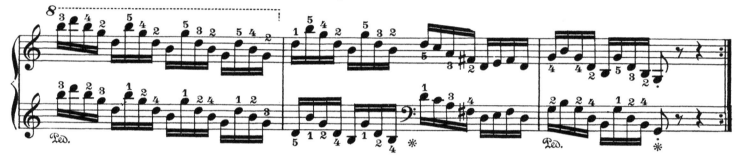

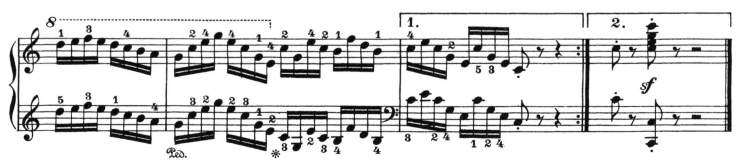

Allegro vivo e scherzoso ($\quad$ = 132)

19.

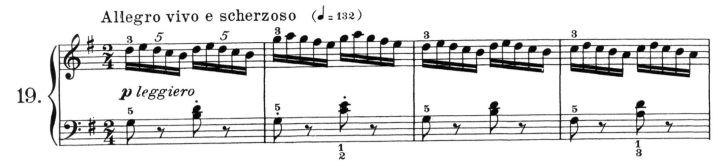

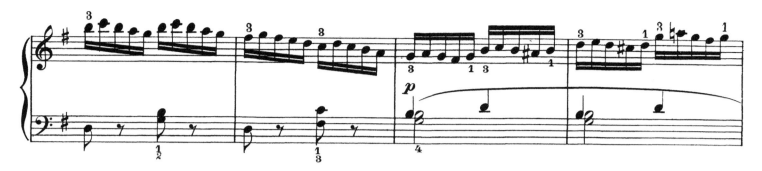

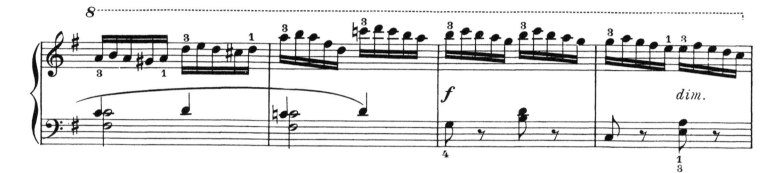

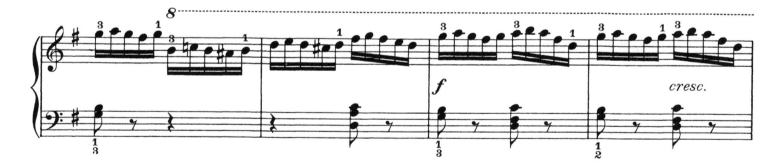

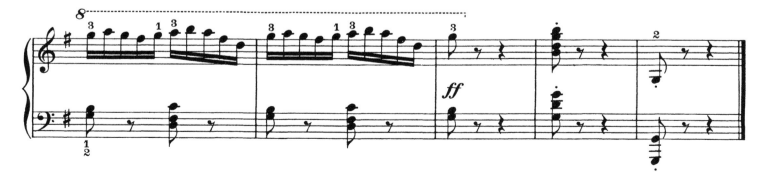

20.

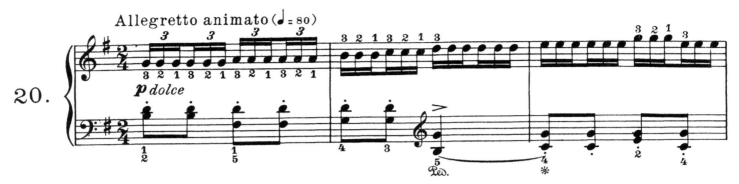

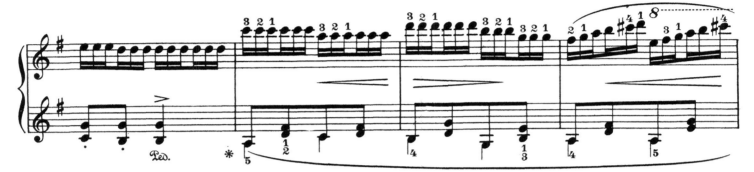

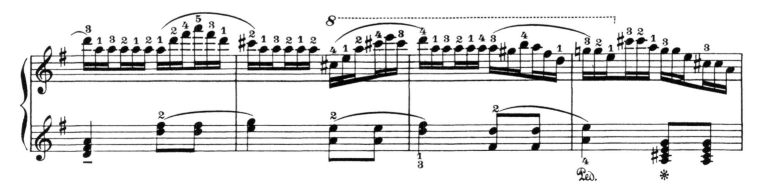

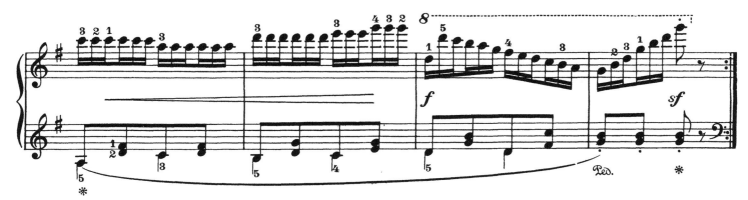

Allegro vivo ($\a. = 112$)

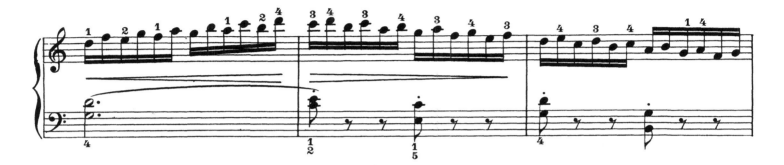

19246

Allegro (♩ = 84)

22.

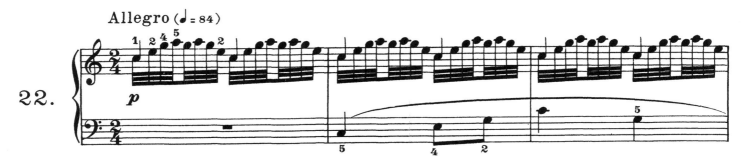

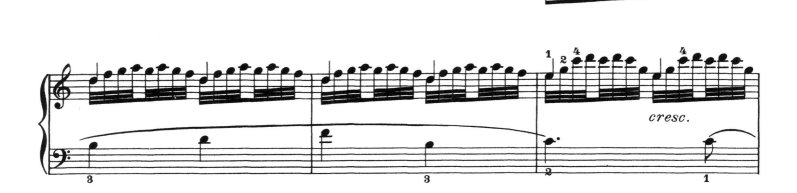

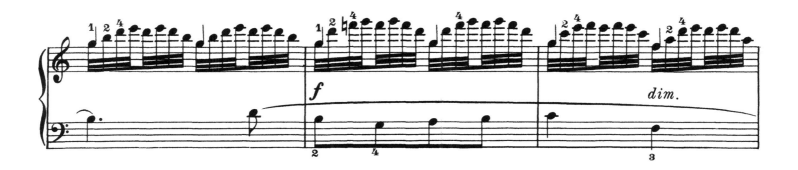

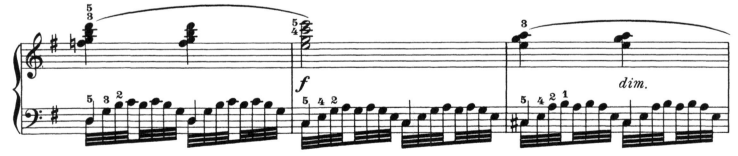

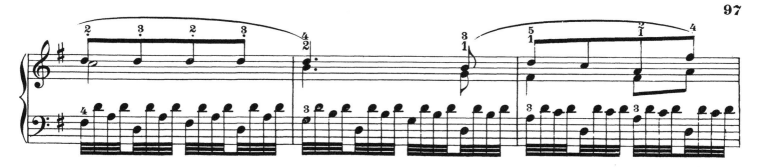

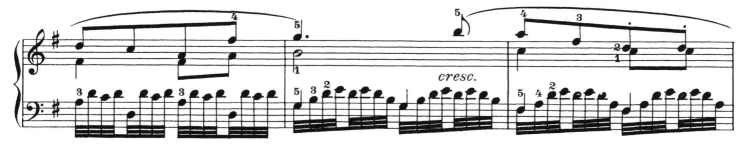

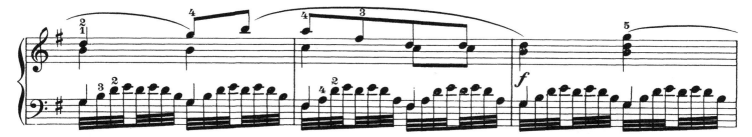

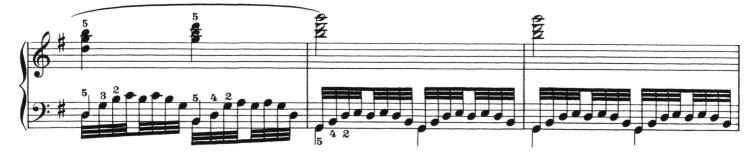

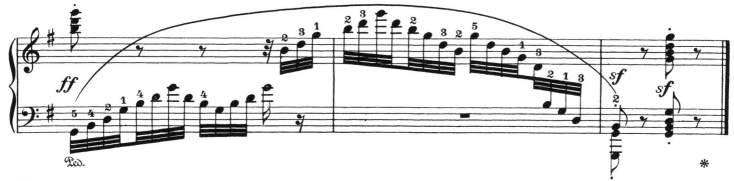

19246

Allegretto vivace

24.

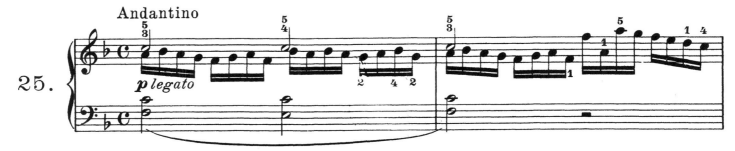

Andantino

25.

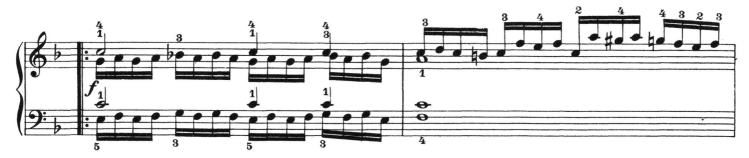

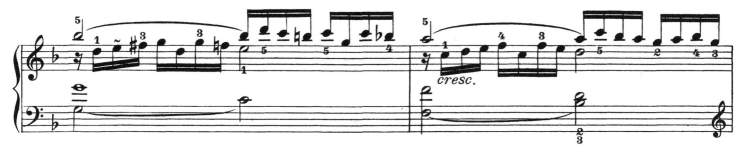

19246

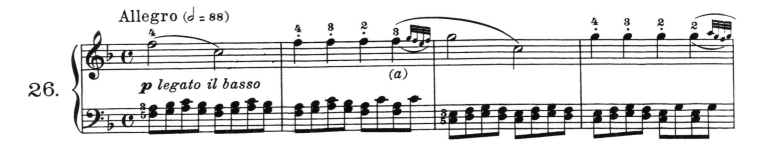

26.

(a) (b) (c) See **a.**

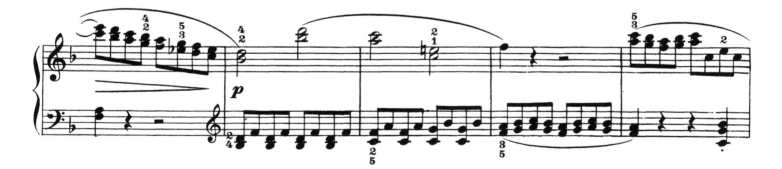

(d)  (e) *See a, page 100*

19246

Allegro moderato ($\quarternote = 108$)

27.

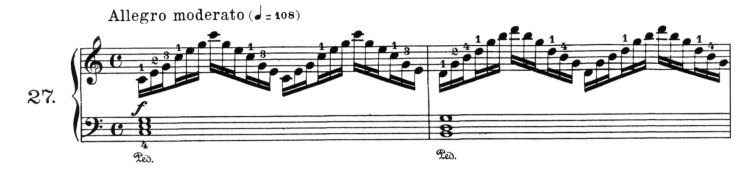

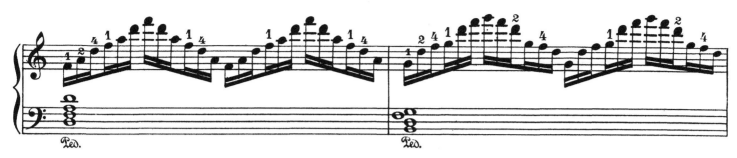

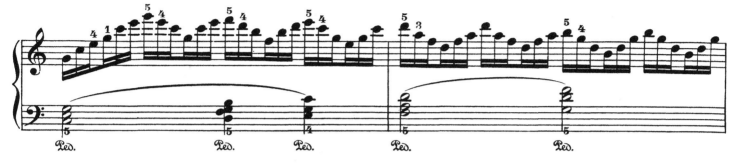

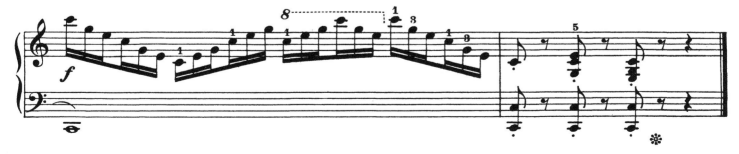

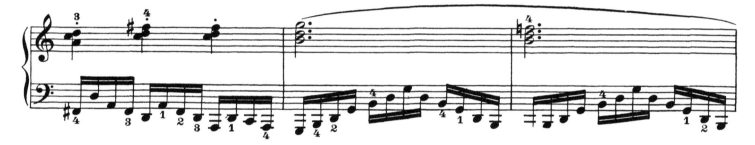

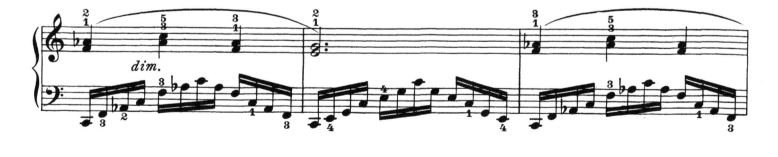

Allegretto

29.

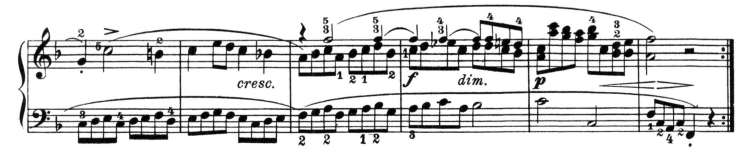

Allegretto

30.

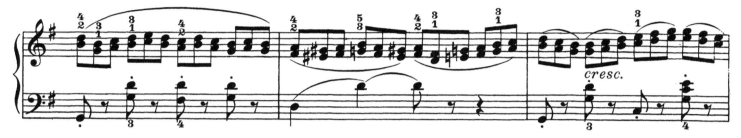

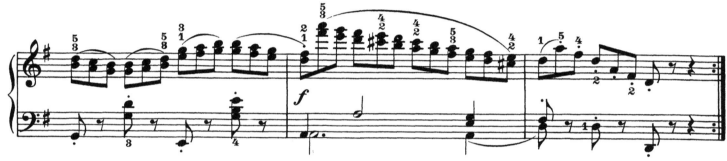

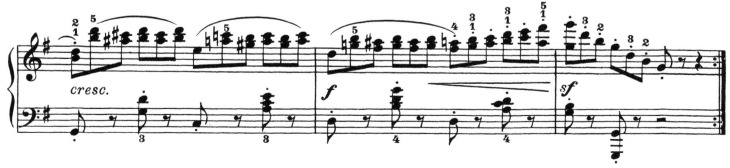

31.

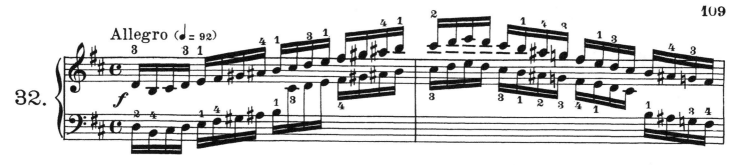

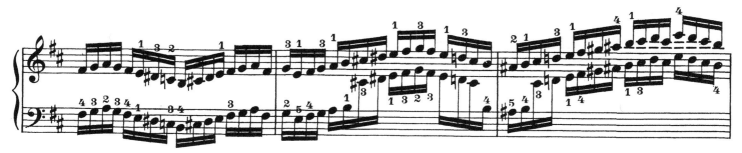

Allegro al galop (♩ = 138)

33.

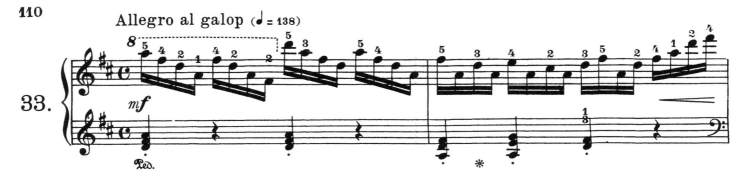

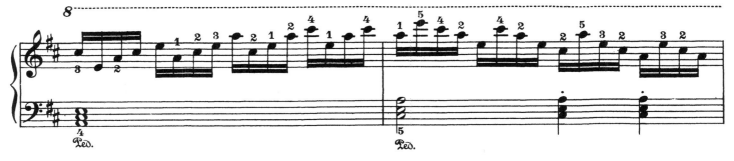

19246

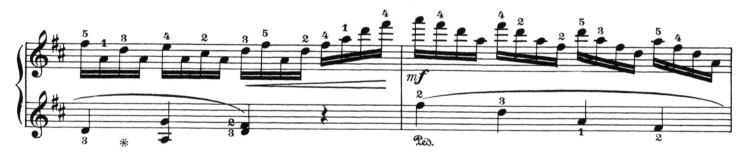

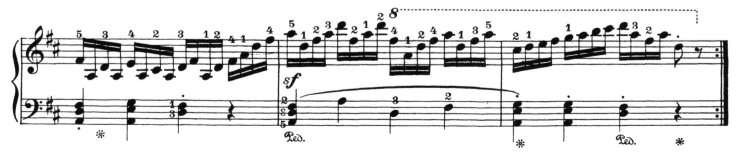

19246

Allegro moderato

34.

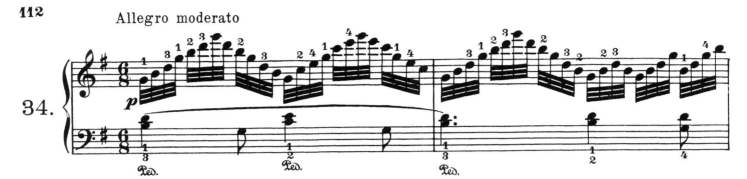

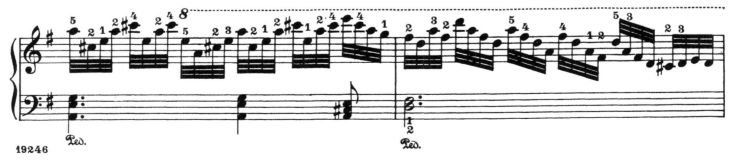

Moderato, sempre tenuto ed arpeggiato

35.

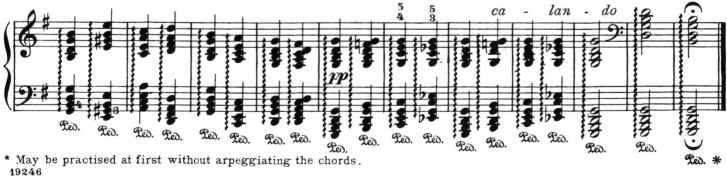

* May be practised at first without arpeggiating the chords.

Allegro moderato e tranquillo

36.

Allegro

37.

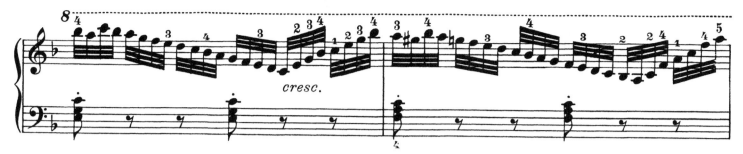

19246

The *Legato* in four-part writing; the hand must be held very quiet, and the fingers must strike simultaneously, without an arpeggio.

41.

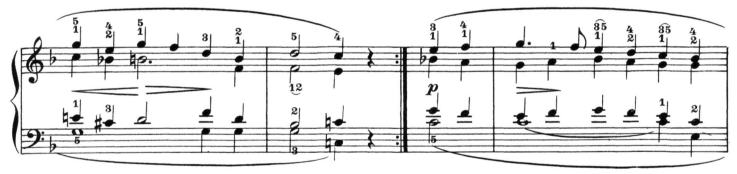

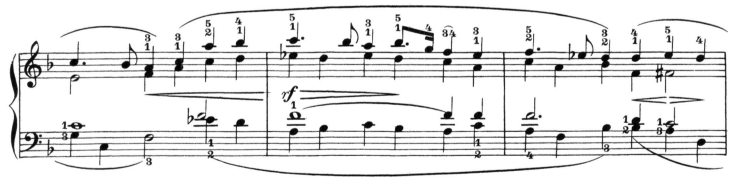

Allegretto vivace (♩=108)

42.

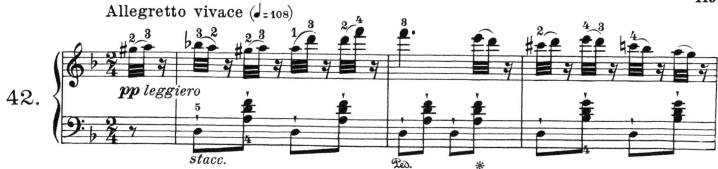

Allegro ($\flat$ = 160)

43:*

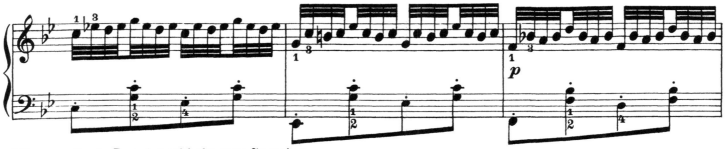

*Also practise in B major, with the same fingering.

19246

Allegretto vivace ($\textstyle\mathbf{J}$ = 92)

44.

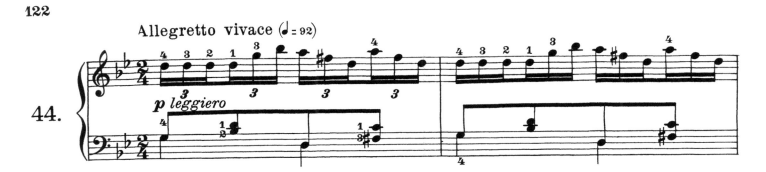

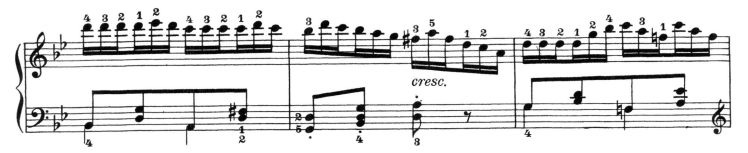

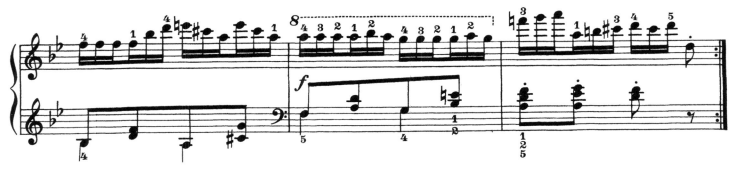

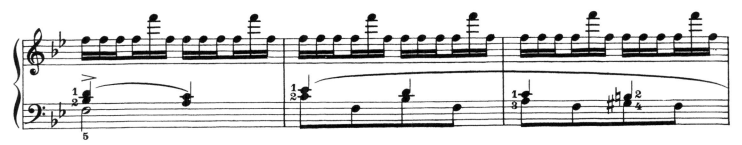

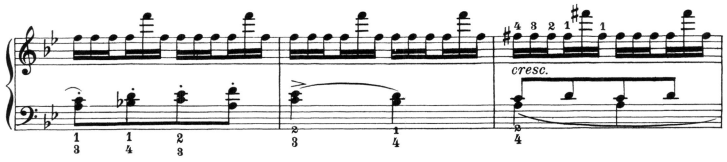

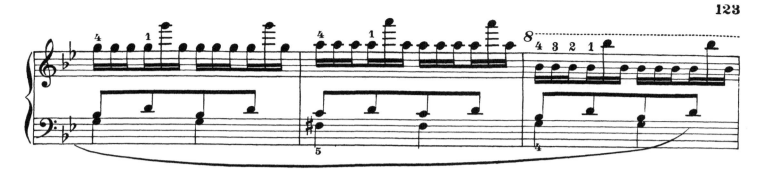

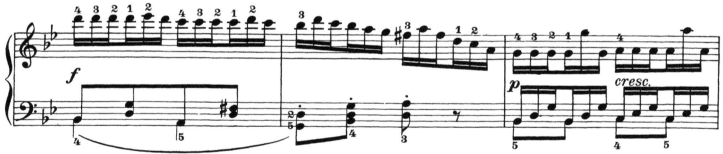

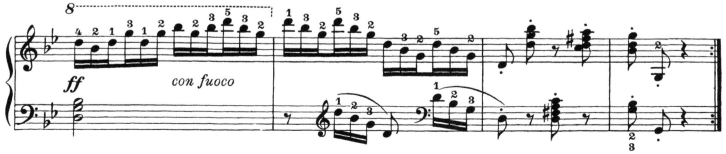

19246

Allegretto

45.

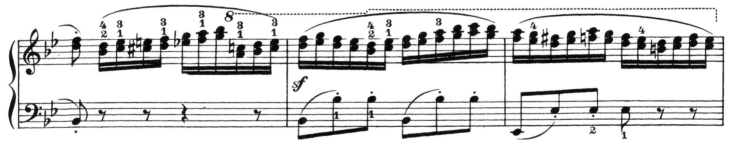

Molto allegro (♩=160)

46.

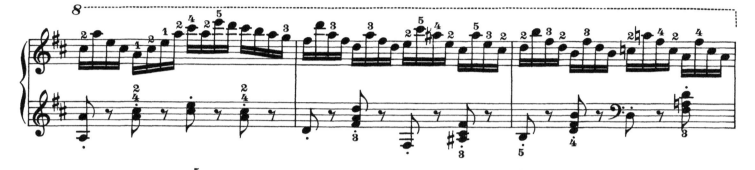

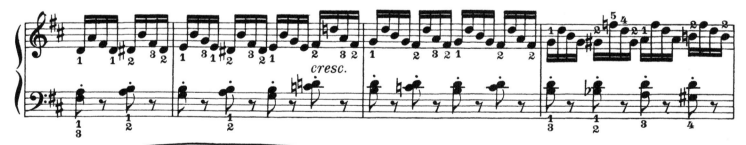

19246

Andantino cantabile
(Preghiera)

47.

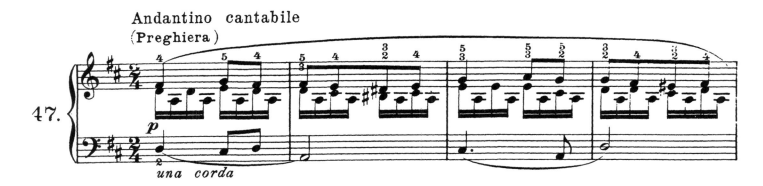

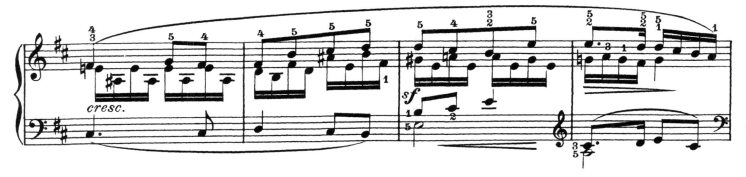

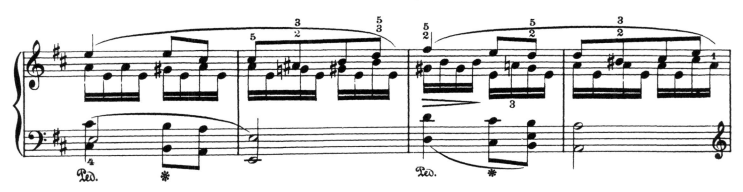

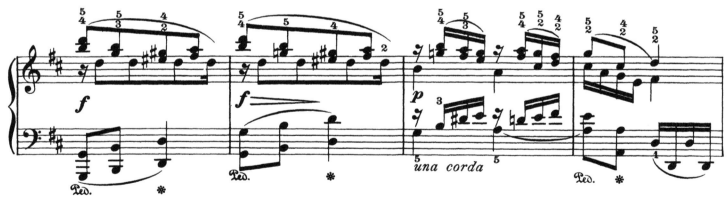

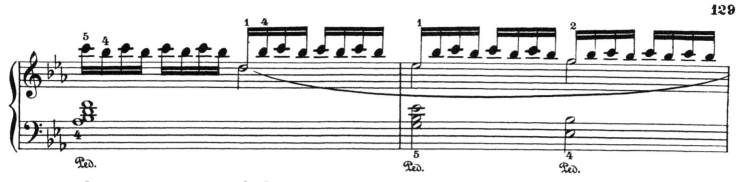

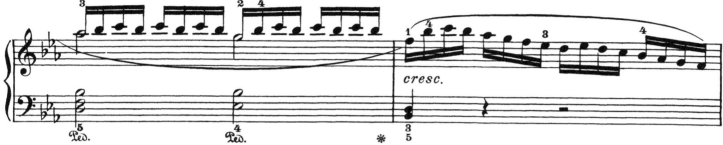

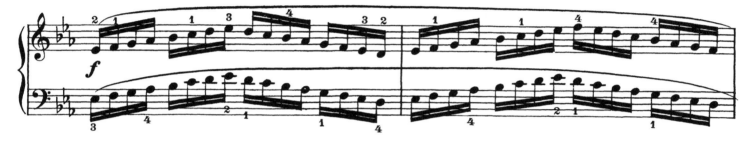

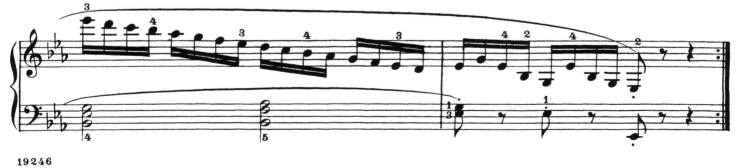

19246

Allegro leggiero (♩=176)

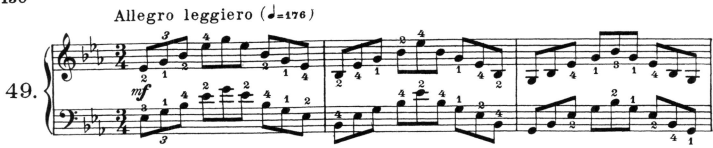

49.

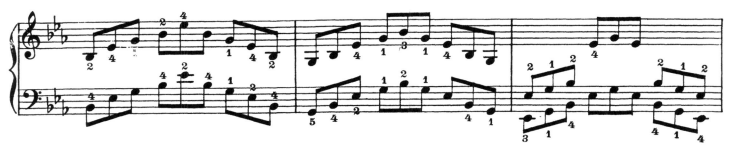

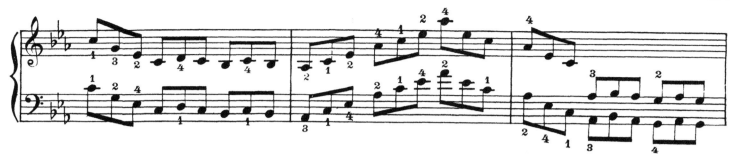

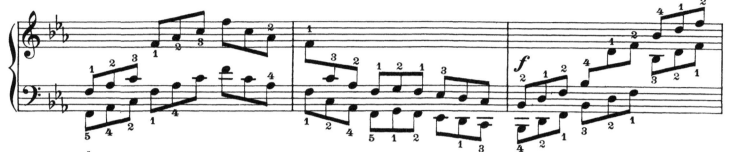

Allegro ($\quarternote = 96$)

50.

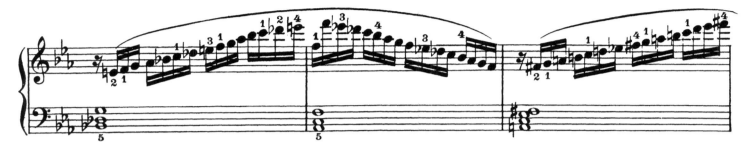

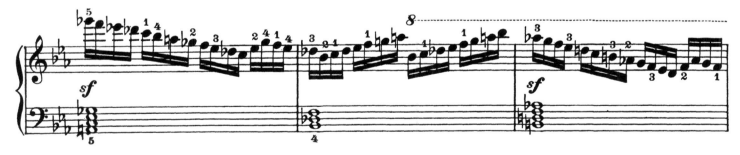

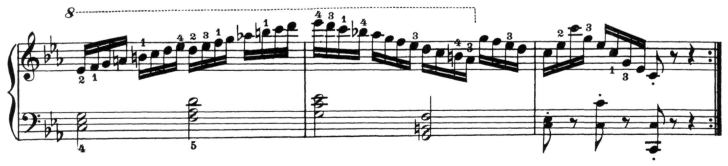

Vivace con fuoco

51.

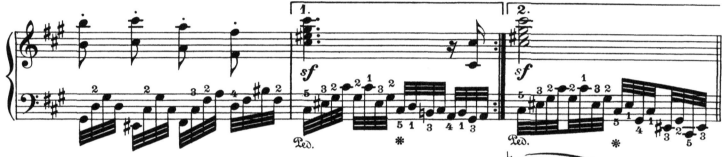

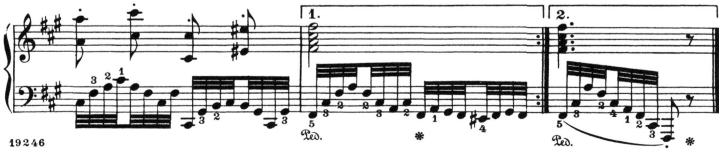

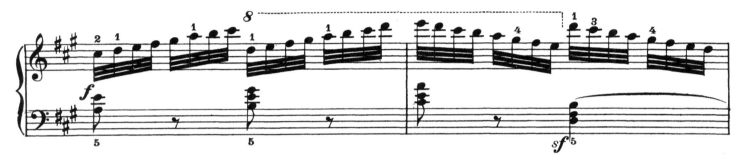

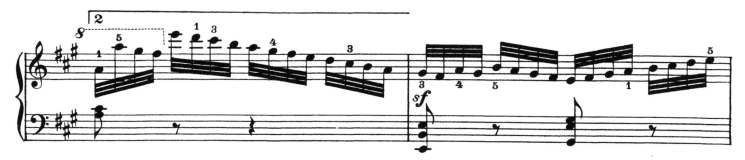

19246

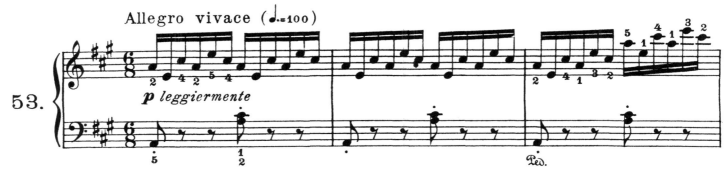

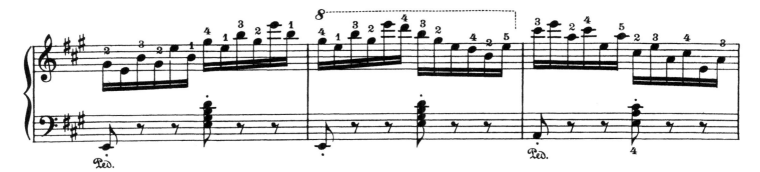

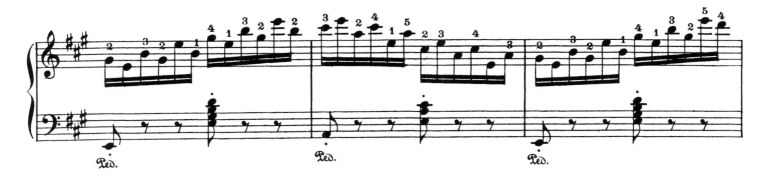

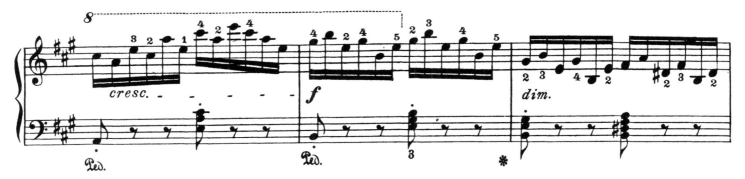

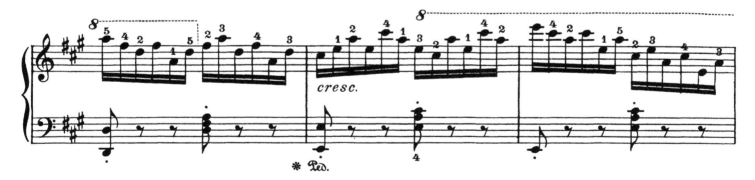

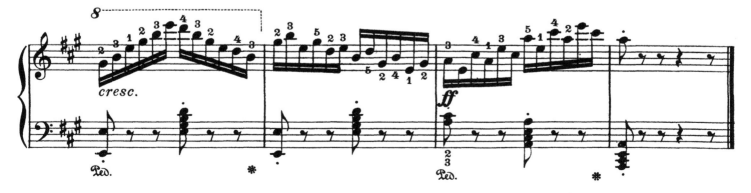

19246

Lento espressivo

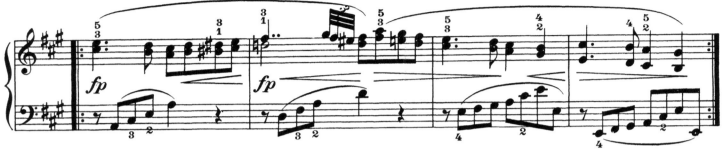

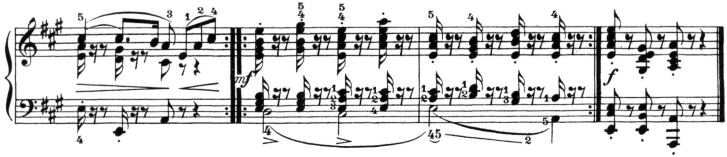

Andante espressivo e cantabile

55.

Preparatory Exercise for Playing Three Notes Against Two.

Allegro commodo (♩ = 132)

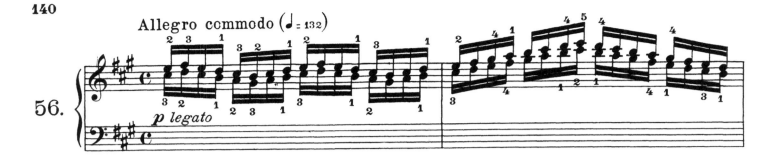

56.

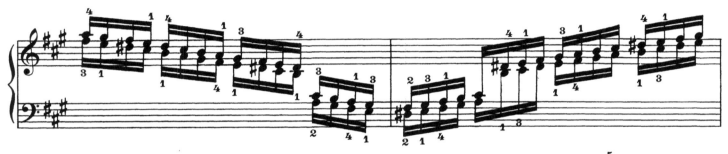

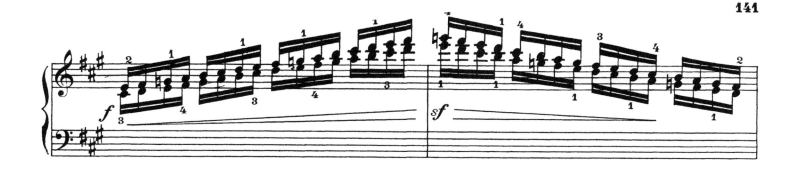

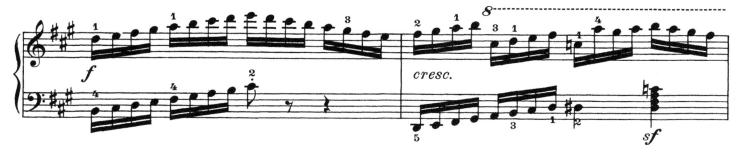

57.

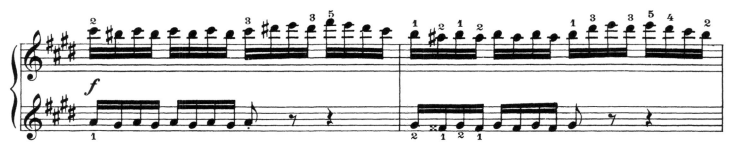

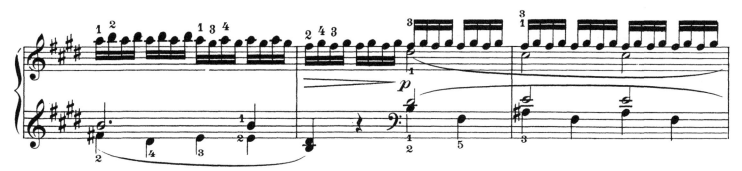

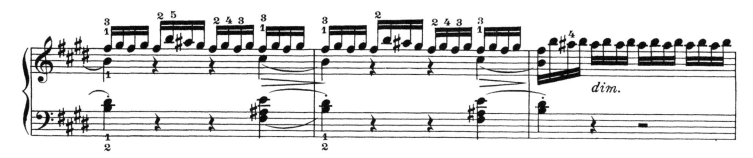

19246

Allegretto vivace (♩= 80)

legato

58.

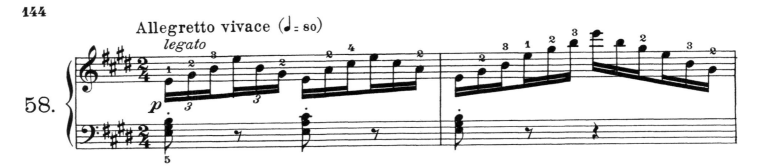

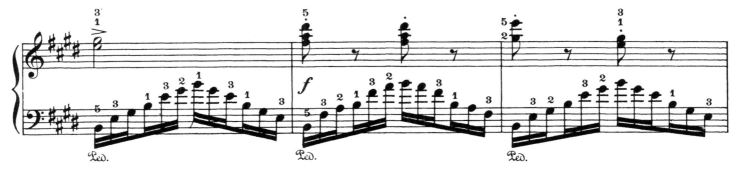

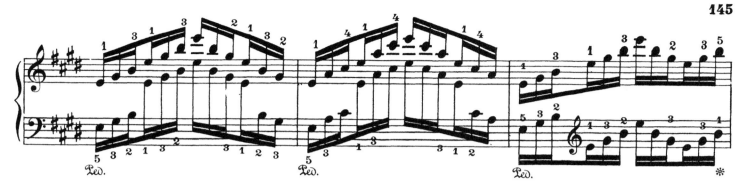

19246

Molto presto

60.

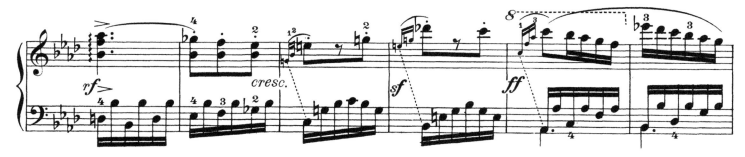

Allegro moderato (♩ = 132)

61*

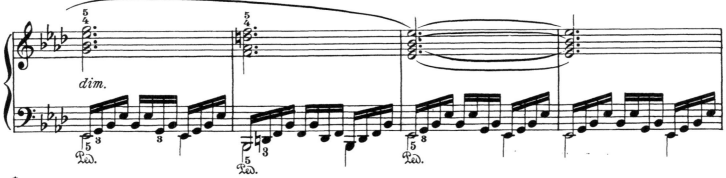

* Also transpose into A major

19246

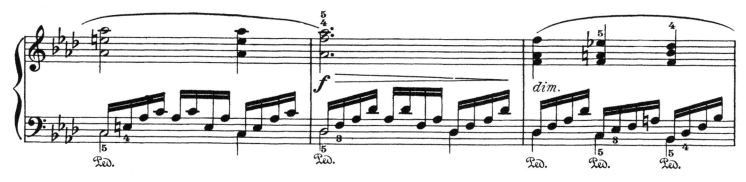

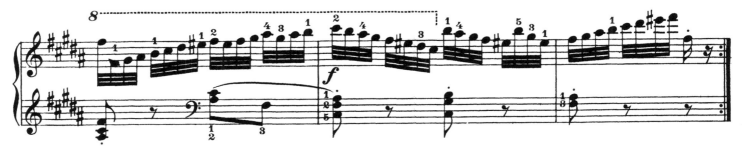

* Original key C major

Allegro.

63.

Allegretto (♩ = 72)

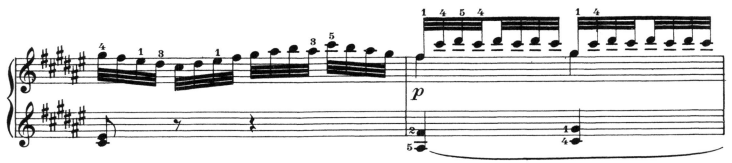

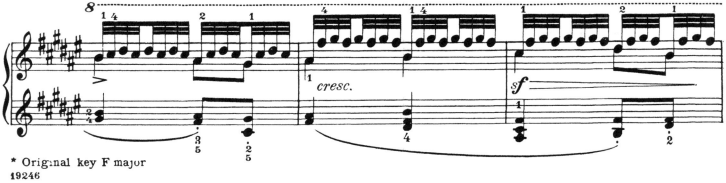

* Original key F major

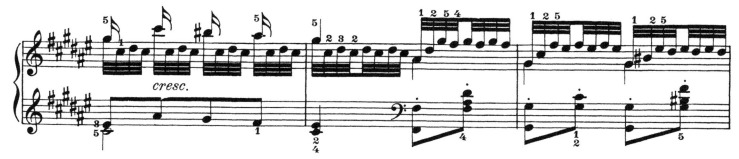

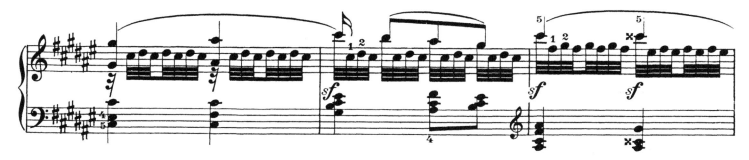

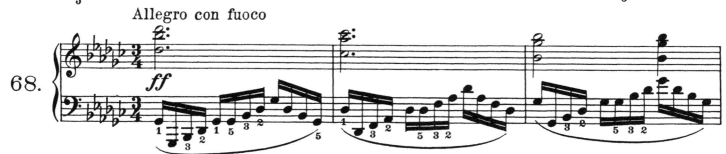

Allegro con fuoco

68.

Allegro moderato

69.

Preparatory Exercise to Octave-Studies on page 162

r.h.

(Left hand two octaves lower)

Allegro risoluto

70 a.

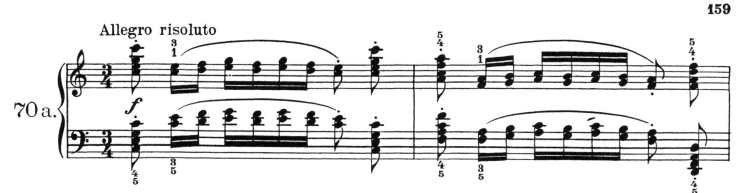

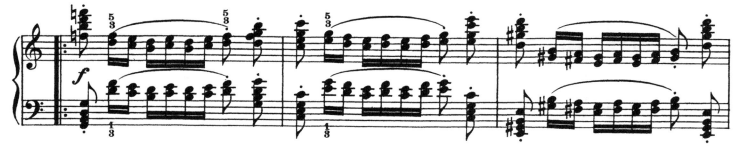

Allegro risoluto (No 70a transposed into C♯ major)

70b.

Allegro risoluto (No 70 a transposed into C♭ major)

70 c.

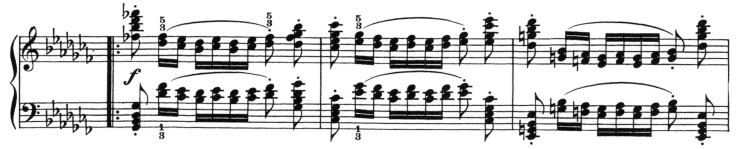

Supplement

Eight Octave-Studies

1.

Variant 1

Variant 2

Presto

2.*

* Practise also with Variants as in No.1

Molto allegro

3.

Allegro moderato

4.

168

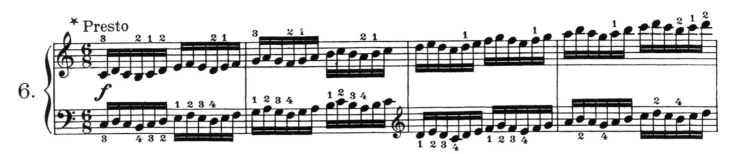

*Practise legato and staccato

Variant 1

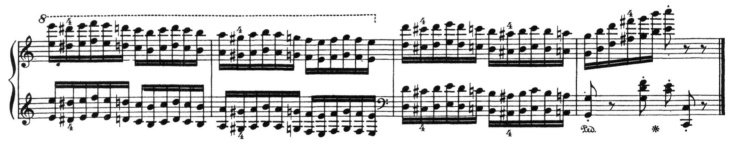

Variant 2

19246

* The original has no octaves